The VIKING Employee

Dedication

To all the warriors who dare to dream big, who refuse to settle for mediocrity, and who believe in the power of their own potential. May this book serve as a reminder of the Viking within you, a spirit that thrives on challenges, embraces growth, and conquers every obstacle with relentless determination.

Preface

In the annals of history, the Vikings stand as a symbol of courage, resilience, and unyielding ambition. Their stories, etched in tales of epic journeys and daring raids, continue to captivate and inspire generations. But beyond the myth and legend lies a profound truth: the Viking spirit is not a relic of the past but a powerful force that resides within each of us.

This book is a journey of self-discovery, an exploration of the Viking within. It is a guide to unlocking the warrior spirit that lies dormant within your soul, waiting to be awakened and unleashed. It is a call to action, an invitation to embrace the values and principles that propelled the Vikings to greatness, and apply them to your own life, both personally and professionally.

Prepare to embark on a transformative odyssey as we delve into the mindset of the Viking, uncovering the secrets that fueled their relentless drive and unwavering commitment to excellence. You will learn to tap into the power of fear, cultivate a sense of ownership, and chart your own course toward a life filled with purpose, achievement, and lasting fulfillment.

This book is not just a collection of motivational words; it's a roadmap to action. It will equip you with the tools and strategies you need to overcome obstacles, conquer your fears, and achieve extraordinary results. It's time to unleash the Viking within and embark on a journey of self-discovery and boundless possibility.

Table of Contents

Introduction

The Viking Within: Unlocking Your Inner Warrior for Success is a journey into the heart of human potential. It's a call to action for those seeking to break free from the ordinary and achieve extraordinary results. It's a guide to embracing the Viking spirit, a potent combination of courage, resilience, and unyielding determination, and harnessing it to achieve success in all areas of your life.

But what exactly is the Viking spirit? It's not just about brute force or aggression. It's a mindset, a way of life, a set of values and principles that fueled the Vikings' relentless drive to conquer the unknown. It's a spirit that thrives on challenges, embraces growth, and conquers every obstacle with unwavering determination.

This book will guide you through the core tenets of the Viking spirit, revealing how they can be applied to your own personal and professional life. You'll learn how to:

Embrace a 'King in Your Own Right' Mentality:
Take control of your destiny, refusing to be defined by others' expectations.

Craft Your Own Destiny:
Set your own course and chart your path to success, based on your unique values and goals.

Prepare for the Unexpected:
Develop adaptability and resilience, embracing uncertainty as an opportunity for growth.

Unleash the Power of Fear:
Recognize the power of fear as a motivator, not a deterrent, and use it to propel you toward greater achievements.

Leave Your Mark:
Create a lasting impact, building a legacy that inspires others.

This book is not a passive read. It's an interactive experience, designed to ignite your passion, challenge your beliefs, and empower you to unleash your inner warrior. It's a call to action, an invitation to embark on a journey of self-discovery and unlock the boundless potential that resides within you.

The Call of the Warrior

The wind howled like a banshee, whipping across the icy plains of Scandinavia. The sky, a canvas of bruised purple and stormy grey, mirrored the fierce spirit of the warriors who stood poised on the edge of the unknown. Their eyes, hardened by countless battles and etched with a steely resolve, held the promise of conquest and glory. These were the Vikings, and their legend was about to be written in the annals of history.

But the Viking spirit wasn't just about brute force and battlefield prowess. It was a mindset, a way of life that thrived on courage, determination, and an unwavering hunger for self-improvement. It was a spirit that transcended the physical realm and touched the very core of human ambition.

You see, the Viking spirit wasn't exclusive to those who sailed the seas and plundered distant shores. It resided within every human being, waiting to be awakened. It was a dormant force, a hidden reservoir of potential that could be harnessed to overcome obstacles, achieve extraordinary feats, and lead a life brimming with purpose.

Imagine, for a moment, a world where you embrace the Viking spirit within yourself. You, too, can become a warrior in the battleground of life, a champion of your own destiny. You can conquer your fears, rise above limitations, and achieve audacious goals. The Viking spirit is a call to action, a clarion call to unleash the warrior within.

It's a call to break free from the shackles of self-doubt, to cast aside the limiting beliefs that hold you back, and to embrace the power of a growth mindset. It's a call to step out of your comfort zone and embark on a journey of personal transformation.

But before we delve deeper into the secrets of the Viking spirit, let's take a moment to understand its origins. Let's embark on a journey back in time, to a world where the Vikings ruled the seas and carved their legacy into the fabric of history.

The Vikings were a people of unparalleled courage and determination. They were fearless explorers, skilled navigators, and fierce warriors who carved their destiny with a blend of ferocity and ingenuity. They dared to venture into uncharted territories, facing both the allure and perils of the unknown.

"

Their stories, etched in sagas and inscribed on ancient stones, are testament to their remarkable achievements. They sailed across vast oceans, forging trade routes and establishing settlements across Europe. They were renowned for their seafaring skills, their craftsmanship, and their unwavering spirit.

The Viking spirit was forged in the crucible of hardship and adversity. They faced harsh winters, brutal storms, and relentless enemies. Yet, through it all, they persevered, their resilience and determination serving as an inspiration for generations to come.

But what was it about the Vikings that made them so exceptional? What were the core values that fueled their success?

At the heart of the Viking spirit lay a potent blend of strength and ingenuity. They were warriors, but they were also skilled artisans, farmers, and traders. They embraced a spirit of self-reliance, taking pride in their ability to forge their own destinies and overcome obstacles through their own strength and ingenuity.

Their values, enshrined in the sagas and echoed in their actions, offered a powerful blueprint for success. They believed in honor, courage, loyalty, and a relentless pursuit of excellence. They were not afraid to face their fears, and they embraced challenges as opportunities for growth.

But how can we, in the modern world, tap into this reservoir of Viking spirit? How can we harness these values and apply them to our own lives?

And this is where our journey begins. We will explore the key tenets of the Viking spirit, translating their timeless wisdom into practical strategies for achieving success in your career and personal life.

We will examine the power of mindset, the importance of self-belief, and the art of overcoming limiting beliefs. We will delve into the importance of personal responsibility, self-reliance, and forging your own path.

We will learn how to navigate the storms of uncertainty, embracing challenges as opportunities for growth. We will discover the power of fear, not as a deterrent but as a catalyst for achieving greatness.

And finally, we will explore the warrior's legacy, leaving our own mark on the world by embracing the Viking spirit as a lifelong pursuit of excellence.

So, are you ready to embrace the Viking within? Are you ready to unleash the warrior spirit that lies dormant within you? If so, then join me on this journey of personal transformation.

We will navigate the uncharted waters together, face our fears head-on, and emerge as champions of our own destinies.

But before we begin, let's first examine the foundations of the Viking spirit. Let's look at the values that fueled their success and how these principles can empower us to achieve extraordinary things in our own lives.

In the next chapter, we'll explore the legacy of the Vikings, their values, and their achievements. We'll uncover the secrets of their success and how these timeless principles can be applied to the challenges and opportunities of the modern world.

But for now, let this call to action resonate within you. Feel the energy of the Viking spirit coursing through your veins, and prepare to embark on a journey of self-discovery and transformation. Because within each of us lies the potential for greatness, waiting to be unleashed.

The King in Your Own Right

Jarl was gazing at the cloudy sunset, a young warrior with a steely glint in his eye, his face etched with determination. He had just received his own longships as a gift from his father, the chieftain, and he was on his maiden voyage, a voyage of discovery and self-reliance.

This journey wasn't simply about plundering foreign lands or seeking glory in battle. It was about something deeper, something more profound – a journey of self-discovery. Jarl was ready to step out from under the shadow of his father and become a King in his own right.

As you embark on your own journey of self-discovery, embracing the Viking spirit, you'll find yourself asking similar questions. Who are you? What are your strengths and weaknesses? What truly matters to you?

For the Vikings, individual accomplishment and self-reliance were paramount. They understood that while their community was strong, ultimately, their fate lay in their own hands. Jarl, on his maiden voyage, had to rely on his own judgment, his own skills, and his own courage to navigate the treacherous waters and face any challenges that came his way.

The same is true for you. The Viking spirit is not just about fighting battles or conquering enemies; it's about taking control of your own life, setting your own course, and forging your own path to success.

In this chapter, we'll explore the principles of cultivating ownership and purpose, embracing the power of independence, and building your own kingdom, all driven by the Viking spirit of self-reliance and resilience.

Section 1: Cultivating Ownership and Purpose

The first step towards becoming a King in your own right is taking ownership of your life. This doesn't mean being selfish or arrogant; it means embracing responsibility for your choices and actions.

Think of it this way: The Viking warriors were not simply pawns in their leader's game. They were individuals with their own goals and aspirations, and they fought for their own glory. They were not afraid to stand up for what they believed in, and they took pride in their own accomplishments.

You, too, have the power to shape your own destiny.

You can start by asking yourself:

What are my goals?

What truly matters to me?

What am I passionate about?

Once you have a clear understanding of your values and goals, you can begin to take ownership of your life.

Setting Clear Boundaries

An important part of cultivating ownership is setting clear boundaries. This means being willing to say "no" to things that don't align with your values or goals. It means refusing to be defined by others' expectations.

Think about the Viking warriors. They had clear boundaries with their enemies. They knew who they were fighting and what they were fighting for. They were not afraid to stand their ground and defend what was theirs.

You, too, can set clear boundaries in your own life. Say "no" to requests that don't serve you. Don't let others dictate your path or your priorities.

Embracing Responsibility

Taking ownership also means embracing responsibility for your choices and actions. This doesn't mean blaming yourself for everything that goes wrong, but it does mean recognizing that you have the power to influence your own outcomes.

Imagine Jarl facing a storm at sea. He could blame the weather for his misfortune, or he could acknowledge the challenges he faced, adapt his strategy, and navigate through the tempest.

The same principle applies to your life. Take responsibility for your actions, both good and bad. Don't be afraid to make mistakes, but learn from them and move forward with newfound wisdom.

Section 2: The Power of Independence

The Viking spirit is deeply rooted in independence and self-reliance. They were not dependent on others to provide for them or to make decisions for them. They were skilled warriors, skilled navigators, and skilled craftsmen, able to rely on their own abilities to survive and thrive.

You, too, can harness the power of independence by:

Building a Strong Foundation of Skills and Knowledge

The Vikings were known for their mastery of a wide range of skills. They were skilled shipbuilders, seafarers, warriors, and craftspeople. They understood that the more skills they had, the more adaptable and resilient they could be.

Invest in your own skill development. Learn new things, expand your knowledge, and build a strong foundation of skills that can help you navigate the challenges of life.

Overcoming Obstacles Through Determination and Perseverance

The Vikings were not afraid of obstacles. In fact, they embraced challenges as opportunities for growth. They were determined to overcome any obstacle in their path, and they persevered through hardship with unwavering resolve.

The Viking spirit teaches us that perseverance is key to achieving our goals. There will be obstacles along the way, but it's important to stay focused, to keep going, and to never give up on our dreams.

Section 3: Building Your Own Kingdom

The ultimate goal of embracing the Viking spirit is to build your own kingdom – not a physical kingdom of land and riches, but a kingdom of purpose, fulfillment, and success.

Defining Your Unique Strengths

The Viking warriors were known for their unique strengths. Some were skilled swordsmen, while others were masters of archery. They understood their strengths and they used those strengths to their advantage.

Identify your unique strengths and talents. What are you good at? What are you passionate about? Once you know what your strengths are, you can focus on leveraging them to achieve your goals.

Nurturing a Strong Network of Allies

The Vikings were not lone wolves. They relied on their communities and their networks of allies to achieve their goals. They understood the importance of building strong relationships and of working together.

Build a network of allies and supporters who can help you on your journey. Find mentors, partners, and friends who can provide support, guidance, and encouragement.

Creating Your Own Path

The Vikings were not afraid to forge their own paths. They were not content to follow the same old routines or to simply conform to the expectations of others. They were driven by a desire to create something new, something different, something that would leave a lasting mark on the world.

Be bold and create your own path. Don't be afraid to break the mold and to chart your own course.

Remember this: The Viking spirit is not about conquering others. It's about conquering yourself. It's about finding your inner strength, embracing your individuality, and creating a life filled with purpose, fulfillment, and success.

"Jarl, what are you going to do with your new longships?" asked the chieftain, his father.

Jarl, his face radiating ambition, looked up from the map he was studying. "I am going to explore the uncharted waters," he declared, "to find new lands, to make my own mark on the world."

The chieftain smiled, but a shadow crossed his eyes. "But Jarl, those waters are dangerous. The winds are fickle, and the storms are fierce. Are you prepared for the challenges that await you?"

Jarl straightened his shoulders, his voice filled with confidence. "Father, I am ready. I am not afraid."

The chieftain nodded, a flicker of pride in his eyes. "Then go, my son, and become the King in your own right. Go forth, and make your own destiny."

Jarl, his heart ablaze with ambition, embraced his father, and then, with a resolute nod, he turned and strode towards the deck, his gaze fixed on the horizon.

The journey ahead would be long and arduous, but Jarl was ready. He knew that the power of independence, the spirit of self-reliance, was within him, and he was determined to conquer any challenges that lay ahead.

But as the longship plunged into the waves, a strange feeling washed over him. A sense of unease, of foreboding. The winds seemed to whisper something, a warning, a threat. He looked up at the swirling clouds above, and for the first time, he questioned whether he was truly prepared.

The voyage had just begun, and already, he was facing his first real test. And what lay beyond the horizon? What dangers lurked in the uncharted waters?

The Uncharted Waters

The ship, a magnificent vessel carved from the heart of an ancient oak, cut through the waves with a strength born of both wood and will. Her sails, billowing like the breath of a storm, carried her onward, ever onward, towards an horizon both familiar and unknown. At the helm stood Jarl, a seasoned sailor, his eyes scanning the vast expanse of water, his hands weathered and wise, guiding the ship through the relentless push and pull of the currents.

This was no ordinary voyage. This was a journey into the Uncharted Waters, a metaphor for the unpredictable path that life throws at us all. As we discussed in the previous chapters, embracing the Viking spirit meant not only claiming your rightful place as a king in your own right but also cultivating an unwavering adaptability, a resilience in the face of storms, both literal and metaphorical.

In the heart of the modern world, the Uncharted Waters are as formidable as they ever were. The landscape of careers is shifting like sands on a beach. New technologies emerge, demanding new skills and new ways of thinking. Competition is fierce, and the playing field is constantly being reshaped. The familiar moorings of stability that once anchored us are now a distant memory.

But fear not, Viking warrior! The spirit of the Northmen, as always, offers a beacon of hope in these turbulent times. The key to navigating these uncharted waters lies in embracing a mindset of constant growth and continuous learning. It's about developing the skills to adapt, the resilience to weather the storms, and the vision to chart a course towards a future filled with opportunity.

Let's dive deeper into the Art of Adaptability, a crucial aspect of the Viking spirit. Imagine Jarl, at the helm, his keen eyes trained on the horizon. He's not simply sailing towards a predefined destination, he's navigating a constantly shifting landscape, adjusting his course as needed, embracing the unexpected, and learning from every change in the wind.

The same is true for you, my friend. In the modern world, your career is not a fixed destination; it's a journey, an ongoing exploration of possibilities. Your knowledge, your skills, your very approach to work must be dynamic, ever-evolving, ready to adapt to the changing tides of the marketplace.

Think of it this way: You are building a portable skillset. A set of skills that can be applied across different industries, different roles, and different situations. It's about acquiring knowledge that transcends specific disciplines, about developing a versatility that allows you to thrive in any environment.

This isn't a call to become a jack of all trades, master of none. It's about cultivating a deep understanding of your core strengths and then actively seeking out opportunities to expand your skillset, to learn new technologies, to explore new industries, to continually challenge yourself.

Picture this: You're a software developer working at a large corporation. The job is comfortable, the pay is good, and you're surrounded by colleagues. But a storm is brewing on the horizon: Artificial Intelligence. The rise of AI threatens to automate many of the tasks you currently perform. Instead of succumbing to fear, embrace it as a motivator! Dive headfirst into the world of AI, learn how to work with it, how to leverage its power to enhance your own capabilities. Transform your fear into fuel for growth!

And here's the beauty of it all: Just as Jarl's ship could sail to any destination, your adaptable skillset opens up a world of possibilities. You are not confined to a single career path, you are not chained to a single industry. You are a Viking warrior, free to explore, to adapt, to thrive in the face of any challenge!

Of course, navigating the Uncharted Waters requires more than just adaptability. It also requires a clear vision, a roadmap for success. You need to know where you want to go, what you want to achieve. And for this, you need to understand yourself, your values, your goals.

This is the essence of Charting Your Course, the third and final section of this chapter. Just like Jarl, with his years of experience and his knowledge of the stars, you must develop a long-term vision for your career and your personal life.

Think about your passions, your strengths, your unique contribution to the world. What are you truly good at? What brings you joy? What are your long-term aspirations?

Once you have a clear understanding of your inner compass, you can begin to create a roadmap for success. This roadmap is not a rigid plan, it's a dynamic guide, a framework for your journey. It's a series of checkpoints, milestones, and goals that help you stay focused and ensure that you're heading in the right direction.

But remember, even the most detailed roadmap needs to be regularly assessed and adjusted. The Uncharted Waters are constantly shifting, and you need to be able to react to the changes, to adapt your course, to stay flexible and responsive to the winds of fortune.

We'll explore the process of creating your personal roadmap in the coming chapters.

But for now, let me ask you this: What are your ambitions? What dreams are you willing to chase, what challenges are you willing to conquer? The Uncharted Waters are calling, and the Viking within you is ready to answer.

The Power of Fear

The wind howled like a banshee, whipping icy spray across the deck of the longship. Thorsten, the ship's captain, stood at the helm, his eyes narrowed against the biting cold. His crew, faces etched with concern, huddled together, their breaths forming puffs of white smoke in the frigid air.

They were caught in a storm, a ferocious tempest that threatened to swallow their vessel whole. The waves, monstrous and unforgiving, crashed over the bow, threatening to capsize them. Fear, a chilling presence, coiled around the hearts of the men.

Yet, amidst the chaos, a strange calm descended upon Thorsten. He knew fear. He knew its icy grip, the way it could freeze you in place, rendering you helpless. But he also knew its power as a motivator, a catalyst for action.

"Fear is a double-edged sword," he had once been told by an elder Viking, his voice rough like the bark of a weathered oak. "It can paralyze you, or it can drive you to unimaginable heights." Thorsten understood. Fear, like the wild sea itself, could be both destructive and magnificent. It was the choice of the warrior to decide which power they would wield.

He gripped the helm tighter, his face set with grim determination. He would not let fear conquer him. He would not allow it to cripple his resolve. He would harness its power, transforming it into a weapon against the storm.

"Steady, men!" he roared, his voice a powerful beacon against the wind. "We will weather this. We are Vikings. We are warriors!"

The crew, inspired by his courage, straightened their backs and responded with a fierce yell, their voices echoing against the storm. They worked together, tirelessly, their muscles burning, their bodies aching. They bailed water, secured sails, and fought to keep the ship afloat.

Fear still lingered, a constant companion, but Thorsten had shown them a way to overcome it. He had shown them that fear, when embraced and harnessed, could become a force for survival, a source of strength.

This, you see, is the essence of the Viking spirit. It is not about the absence of fear. It is about the ability to face your fears head-on, to recognize their power, and to transform them into a catalyst for growth and achievement.

Fear is a powerful force, a primal instinct that has guided humanity since the dawn of time. It is the instinct that makes us jump back from danger, that makes us avoid the unknown. But fear, in its purest form, is simply an alarm bell, a warning signal that something is wrong. It is up to us to decide how we respond to that alarm.

Paralyzing fear, the kind that makes us freeze and shrink from challenges, is born of doubt and uncertainty. It is the voice of the timid, the whisper of the insecure. It tells us we are not capable, that we are not strong enough, that we are not worthy.

Healthy fear, on the other hand, is a motivator, a spark that ignites our courage and drives us to overcome obstacles. It is the voice of the warrior, the whisper of the brave. It tells us to be vigilant, to be prepared, to be ready to face whatever challenges lie ahead.

The Vikings, with their daring raids and relentless explorations, understood this power of fear. They did not shy away from it. They embraced it, using it as fuel to push themselves beyond their limits. They understood that fear was a natural part of life, something that could not be eradicated. Instead, they learned to coexist with it, to use it to their advantage.

When a Viking warrior faced a fearsome opponent, he did not shrink back in terror. He did not allow fear to paralyze him. Instead, he drew upon its energy, using it to fuel his attack, to make him stronger, faster, more ferocious.

Fear was not something to be feared, but something to be respected, a force to be channeled and harnessed.

Imagine, for a moment, a Viking warrior standing before a fearsome dragon. The dragon, its scales shimmering like gold, breathes a fiery breath, engulfing the warrior in a wall of flame. The heat sears his skin, the stench of sulfur fills his nostrils. The warrior, his body burning, his heart pounding, might feel a pang of fear. But this fear is not crippling. It is not the paralyzing fear that makes him want to flee. It is the fear that fuels his resolve, that makes him rise to the challenge.

He draws his sword, his muscles tensed, his eyes blazing with defiance. He faces the dragon, not with reckless abandon, but with controlled aggression, with the knowledge that fear is a powerful force, a force he can control.

The same holds true for you. You, too, have a Viking within you, a warrior who is capable of facing your fears and transforming them into a force for good. It is not about becoming fearless. It is about learning to embrace fear, to use it as a motivator, to push yourself beyond your comfort zone, and to achieve your goals.

Fear is a powerful force. But you are more powerful.

"So, how do we conquer our fears? How do we use them to propel us forward? Let's find out." I ask the audience. "And in doing so, we will find a way to become the best versions of ourselves." I pause for a moment, allowing the words to sink in. "But first, I want to share a story with you."

I take a deep breath, steeling myself for the task ahead. It's a story about a man named Lars, a man who overcame his fear of public speaking, the fear that held him back for years.

"Lars was a brilliant engineer, a man with an exceptional mind and a wealth of knowledge. He was a master of his craft, able to solve complex problems with ease. But when it came to speaking in public, he froze. His heart would race, his palms would sweat, his voice would tremble. He would stumble over his words, his mind would go blank. The thought of speaking in front of others filled him with dread."

"He tried everything to overcome his fear. He practiced in front of the mirror, he joined a Toastmasters club, he even sought professional help. But nothing seemed to work. The fear always returned, its grip tighter than ever."

"One day, Lars was given a chance to present his latest invention to a group of investors. It was a chance of a lifetime, an opportunity to secure funding for his groundbreaking work. But the fear was overwhelming. He knew he had to face it, but he couldn't imagine how."

"He sat in his office, the weight of his fear crushing him. He felt trapped, his dreams slipping through his fingers. Then, he remembered something his grandfather had once told him. "Fear is a liar," his grandfather had said. "It tells you you are not capable, that you are not strong enough. But it's a lie. You are capable. You are strong. You are worthy."

"Lars took a deep breath, his mind clearing. He realized that his fear was not a reflection of his true self. It was a false narrative, a story his mind had been telling him for years. He had to change the story."

"He spent the next few days focusing on his strengths, reminding himself of his accomplishments, of his intelligence, of his passion. He visualized himself presenting with confidence, with clarity, with enthusiasm. He practiced, but not with the goal of becoming perfect, but with the goal of becoming comfortable with his own vulnerability."

"When the day of the presentation arrived, Lars was still nervous, but he felt a newfound sense of control. He knew his fear was still there, but he was no longer afraid of it. He had learned to coexist with it, to use it as a motivator, to push himself forward."

"He walked into the room, his head held high, his eyes filled with confidence. He began his presentation, his voice clear and steady, his words flowing effortlessly. He spoke about his invention, his passion, his dreams, his fears. He was vulnerable, but he was also strong, and he was determined to succeed."

"The investors listened intently, their faces expressions of curiosity and admiration. They saw a man who was not afraid to share his vulnerability, a man who was not afraid to admit his fears. They saw a man who had conquered his demons and emerged stronger, more determined than ever."

"Lars' presentation was a success. He not only secured funding for his invention, but he also inspired others to face their own fears. He became a role model for those who were struggling with crippling fear, a testament to the power of embracing your fears and turning them into a force for good."

"Lars' story is a reminder that we all have a Viking within us, a warrior who is capable of facing our fears and transforming them into a force for good. We can choose to be controlled by our fears, or we can choose to control them. The choice is ours."

I pause for a moment, allowing the audience to absorb the story of Lars. I see the nods of understanding, the glint of recognition in their eyes. They are starting to see the power within themselves, the potential to overcome their own fears.

"So, what are you afraid of?" I ask, my voice echoing through the room. "What fear holds you back? What dream are you afraid to pursue?"

"Think about it for a moment. What is it that keeps you from achieving your goals?"

"It might be the fear of failure, the fear of rejection, the fear of judgment. It might be the fear of the unknown, the fear of stepping outside your comfort zone."

"Whatever it is, know this: You are not alone. We all have fears. But we also have the power to overcome them. We have the power to choose courage over fear. We have the power to become the warriors we were meant to be."

I pause, my eyes scanning the audience, looking for signs of agreement. I see the determination in their eyes, the glimmer of hope. They are ready to face their fears, to embrace the Viking within.

"I want you to think about this: What would a Viking do?" I ask, my voice taking on a more powerful tone. "Would a Viking let fear hold him back? Would a Viking let fear dictate his destiny?"

"No! A Viking would face his fear head-on! He would embrace the challenge! He would harness the power of fear and transform it into a weapon against his enemies!"

"That's what we must do," I say, my voice rising to a crescendo. "We must embrace our fears. We must face them head-on. We must use them as fuel to drive us forward. We must become the warriors we were meant to be!"

"But there's one more thing," I say, my voice softening, my eyes filled with a newfound intensity. "There's one more fear that we must conquer. And that fear, my friends, is the fear of our own greatness."

I see a ripple of confusion in the audience. They are intrigued. They want to know more.

"What is the fear of our own greatness?" I ask, my voice a whisper. "It's the fear that holds us back from achieving our full potential. It's the fear that tells us we are not worthy, that we are not capable, that we are not meant for greatness."

"But the truth is, we are all capable of greatness. We all have the potential to achieve extraordinary things. The only thing holding us back is our own fear. The fear of our own greatness."

"So, what are you waiting for?" I ask, my voice filled with urgency. "What are you afraid of? What are you holding back? It's time to unleash the Viking within. It's time to conquer your fears. It's time to embrace your greatness."

I pause, my words hanging in the air, my eyes locked on the audience. I see the fire in their eyes, the spark of inspiration. They are ready to take the next step. They are ready to unleash the Viking within.

"But before we do," I say, a mischievous glint in my eye, "I have one more story to tell you. It's a story about a Viking named Jarl, a man who was not afraid to dream big, a man who was not afraid to embrace his own greatness."

I take a deep breath, and the story begins to unfold...

The Warriors Legacy

The wind howled through the fjords, carrying with it the scent of salt and the echo of ancient stories. We stand on the precipice of a new chapter in our journey. You've embraced the call of the warrior, cultivated your own kingdom, and learned to navigate the uncharted waters of life. You've stared down fear and emerged stronger, a testament to the Viking spirit that burns within.

But there's more to this journey. The true measure of a warrior isn't solely about personal achievement; it's about leaving a legacy, about inspiring others to ignite their own inner fires. It's about understanding that your life, your journey, is more than just about you. It's about making a difference, about contributing to something bigger than yourself.

Think of the Viking longships, vessels that carried not only warriors but also explorers, traders, and storytellers. They ventured into unknown territories, forging new paths and leaving behind a legacy of courage, adventure, and innovation.

It's the same with you. You have within you the potential to create a legacy, a lasting impact on the world around you.
This is the true warrior's legacy—the ripples of your actions, the stories you leave behind, and the lives you touch.

Section 1: Leaving Your Mark

The world is a vast canvas, and every individual is a brushstroke, adding color and texture to its grand narrative. Your legacy is the masterpiece you create. It's not about being remembered for wealth or power; it's about leaving a mark that resonates, that inspires, and that endures.

Identify Your Unique Contribution

What is your unique contribution to the world? What gifts and talents do you possess that can make a difference?
Perhaps you're an innovator, a visionary, or a gifted storyteller. Maybe you have a knack for teaching, leading, or simply inspiring others.

Think of the legendary Viking explorer, Leif Erikson. He wasn't content with staying in his homeland; he sought new horizons, braved the unknown, and became the first European to set foot on North America. He left behind a legacy of exploration, a testament to human curiosity and the power of venturing beyond known limits.

Living With Purpose

The Viking warriors lived with purpose. They had a clear sense of what they were fighting for, what they believed in, and what they wanted to achieve. This purpose gave them strength and resilience, even in the face of adversity.

You, too, can live with purpose. Think about the things you're passionate about, the causes you believe in, and the impact you want to make. Let your purpose guide your actions, your choices, and your goals.

Consider the story of Ragnar Lothbrok, a Viking warrior whose name is synonymous with courage and determination. He fought for his people, his beliefs, and his land. He left behind a legacy of leadership, a symbol of strength and defiance in the face of overwhelming odds.

Section 2: Continuing the Journey

The warrior's journey never truly ends. It's a lifelong pursuit of growth, of constantly pushing your limits, and of striving for excellence in every aspect of your life.

Embrace Continuous Improvement

The Viking warriors were masters of adaptability. They constantly honed their skills, learned from their experiences, and sought ways to improve. They understood that the journey was never over, that there was always room for growth.

You, too, can embrace a culture of continuous improvement. Stay curious. Seek new challenges. Learn from your mistakes. And never be afraid to step outside your comfort zone.

Think of the Viking raids, not merely as acts of aggression but as opportunities to learn, to gain experience, and to expand their knowledge of the world. Each raid, each battle, presented a chance for growth and improvement.

Inspire Others

Your legacy doesn't end with your own achievements. It's about inspiring others to embrace their own inner warrior, to unleash their potential, and to make a difference in the world.

You have a unique voice, a perspective that can inspire and empower others. Share your knowledge, your stories, and your passion. Be a mentor, a guide, and a source of encouragement for those around you.

Think of the powerful sagas, the tales of Viking heroes that have been passed down through generations, inspiring generations of people with their tales of courage, resilience, and adventure.

Section 3: The Viking Within You

The Viking spirit isn't just a historical relic; it's a powerful force that lives within each of us. It's the drive to overcome challenges, the courage to face fear, and the determination to achieve greatness.

Embrace the Viking spirit in all aspects of your life. Live with purpose. Embrace uncertainty. Develop a growth mindset. And never stop striving for excellence.

Remember, you have the power to leave a legacy that endures. You have the potential to make a difference in the world. The Viking within you is waiting to be unleashed.

"But," a voice whispered from the back of the room, "how do we know if we've truly made a difference? How do we know if our legacy is worth anything?"

"That's a question that will guide us on our journey. It's a question we must ask ourselves every day,""And the answer, my friends, may just lie in the next chapter of our story."

Acknowledgments

Writing a book is a solitary endeavor, but it's one that would be impossible without the support of many incredible people. First and foremost, I want to thank my family and friends for their unwavering belief in me and my vision for this project. Their encouragement and understanding have been invaluable throughout this journey.

I want to thank the countless individuals whose stories and experiences inspired this book. You are the embodiment of the Viking spirit, and your resilience, determination, and pursuit of excellence serve as a beacon of inspiration for us all.

About Author

Tanveer Singh Narray is an IT consultant , corporate employee and a mirror reflection of you "THE READER" . He has a passion for helping individuals unlock their full potential, achieve their goals, and live a life of purpose. This is the writer's first book and if this goes well , he has many more to share.

Tanveer Singh Narray is an avid student of history and is particularly fascinated by the Viking era. Tanveer believes that the Viking spirit of courage, resilience, and independence holds valuable lessons for individuals navigating the challenges of modern life.

Tanveer Singh Narray
resides in Hong Kong and can be found online at
[https://www.linkedin.com/in/tanveerr-singh-narray-91284b30/]